FutureGoldCoin
& Calycoin

President : David Gomadza

Tomorrow's World Order

www.tomorrowsworldorder.com

Info@tomorrowsworldorder.com

FutureGoldCoin

A New World. A New Beginning.
No Wars Ever Again.
No Weapons Ever Again.
No Woman or Child To Die Needlessly.
Sanctions: Banned!
A New World Order.
Fossil Fuels [Oil etc] Banned.
All Fossil-Fuel-Powered Vehicles and Machinery
Banned & To Be Phased Out.
Brand New Renewable Energy Sources.
BRAND NEW LAWS.
No More Torture, Human Rights Violations,
No Genocides, No Crimes Against Humanity. etc .
Only Peace and Networking.

JOIN US TODAY!
A New Chapter.
A New World!!

Powering Tomorrow

DAVID GOMADZA

The current system has crashed and is now obsolete. Only a new system can solve today's global problems. The rise of Tomorrow's World Order.[TWO]

A NEW CHAPTER. CHANGE IS IMMINENT AND INEVITABLE!

TOMORROW'S
WORLD
ORDER

TABLE OF CONTENTS

INTRODUCTION
Why the Need of A Single Reserve Global Currency [SRGC].
Our Solution: The FutureGoldCoin. 8
THE CURRENT PROBLEMS AND OUR SOLUTIONS. 16
FutureGoldCoin 17
Role of A Nation's Sovereignty as the Key to Success. 17
The Current System is Obsolete and Therefore Not Fit for Purpose. 19
Our Plan. 23
Comprehensive Approach. 23
Laws. 23
Ensuring the Right Leadership and Safeguarding the System from
External Forces. 24
The Financial System. 24
Global Reserve Bank. [GRB] 25
Dealing with Current Debt. 26
Nukes in the Hands of a Few But Banning Everyone Else. 27
Sovereignty Risk and Conflicts with Our Laws. 27
Real Idea Behind the IMF and Global Laws. 27
Empowering Every Nation by Providing the Best Framework to Reduce
and Eliminate Side Effects of Our Growth Method. 28
Creating Global Savings. 29
Sole Reason for Government's Existence 30

The Value of Printing Money.	30
Government Mandate to Bail-out Its People.	31
Perpetual Indebtedness.	32
Forever Growth and Building of Wealth.	32
Dealing with Debt. The First Rule is to Offset it.	33
Two Kinds of Debt.	33
Government's 'I owe You' Through Printing New Money.	34
Dealing with External Debt.	34
The Debt Plan.	34
Use of Printed Money.	35
Print Extra Cash to Act as A Buffer to Loan Defaulting.	35
Five-Year Plan Gradually Printing of Money.	35
Supporting Packages.	36
Ban Sanctions.	37
Problem at Hand.	39
Empathy Clause.	41
Humanitarian Grounds.	42
Widen Scope of Punishment.	42
Lack of Understanding of What is Really Needed in Life.	43
Recap: The Solution in Brief.	47
Printing Rights and Licensing for Fiscal Monetary Measures.	48
The Currency as A Hyperinflation Fighter.	48
Levels Never Achieved Before.	49
Your Part.	50
Benefits to You the Investor or Supporter.	51
Reliance on Wars as A Solution to All Problem.	52
PRODUCT/SERVICE/METHODOLOGY.	54

Raising Initial Capital to Kick Start the Project. 54

Your Role. Support Our Initial Token Offering. 54

How Many Tokens for the Initial Offering? 55

Initial Offerings 55

Pre-Sale Offerings. 56

Initial Coin Offerings Kick Off. 56

Guaranteed Tomorrow. 58

NEW SINGLE RESERVE GLOBAL CURRENCY 62

    FutureGoldCoin [FCI]. 62

    Calycoin [CLC]. 62

DETAILED DIGITAL CURRENCY INFORMATION. 64

Distribution Scheme Percentage of Total Supply 72

BUY OUR TOKENS TODAY! 78

I PROMISE YOU VALUE FOR YOUR INVESTMENT! 78

Key Takeaways 79

Table of Abbreviations 81

INTRODUCTION

Why the Need for a Single Reserve Global Currency? [SRGC]

First, the current system is the product of the Bretton Woods System that collapsed in 1971 although it's an improvement on the Bretton Wood's fixed rate exchange theory nevertheless the system is not fit for the purpose. It crashed years ago and only a new system can solve today's global problems. The rise of Tomorrow's World Order [TWO] to oversee and manage the fiscal aspects of this SRGC; the FutureGoldCoin [FCI]; a digital global currency for all international and domestic transactions.

Our Solution: The FutureGoldCoin.

Our FCI will be competing with all global currencies as it will exchange with all currencies and not just by itself which might make it valueless. The effect of exchanging with all currencies will mean increased value beyond any imagination. Our system will enable every country to print new money and never to rely on loans from, e.g. the International Monetary Fund or from other countries. To fight hyperinflation, we will create a Global Reserve Bank [GRB] that will hold each nation's local currency. Every country under our five-year growth and wealth plan will have to print new money free and owe its citizens thereby increasing their value and the wealth of the nation. But all new money will be deposited into our GRB as their savings and we will issue the FCI's equivalent which they will inject into their economy to help fight hyperinflation. Our FCI will be a global digital currency and each country will have to use two currencies. Their own currency and our global digital FCI.

- ✓ Printing is the only source of new money and never loans.
- ✓ New fresh printed money to be deposited into that nation's savings account with us in the GRB.
- ✓ We issue our FCI equivalent value of the new printed money that has been deposited with us and they take this money and inject it into the economy.
- ✓ Every time new fresh money is printed, the nation's government 'owes' its citizens, and that increases their value and the wealth of the economy.
- ✓ Our GRB removes extra or surplus local currency from the economy to control inflation and we hold these for every nation as their savings.
- ✓ Our GRB stimulate a need to create savings and create new wealth.
- ✓ That means our FCI will exchange with all global currencies. They print new money in their local currency, and we take that money into their global savings account we hold for them and issue our global digital FCI to use as an exchange.
- ✓ They use their local currency as well in their economy and might take some new printed money as their local currency depending on circulating levels.
- ✓ To increase the value of FCI, they must stockpile our FCI to upward pressure of our currency as a tool to help fight inflation as they can then export their products cheaper against the FCI.

- ✓ Our system keeps the value of the local currency high. New local currency printed money is used locally only and in surplus reduces in value, but our system will maintain the value of that currency as they deposit some new money with us and get the FCI to use and any extra FCI they can stockpile these in their own country.
- ✓ In inflationary or hyper-inflationary times since they are using two currencies our FCI and their local currencies, they can use our FCI as the price determiner. This is because their own currency might be changing value rapidly, so our digital FCI will be used for pricing.
- ✓ It will be possible as well to stop using their money and deposit it in the GRB with us to fight hyperinflation for some time until they are in control where they can resume using their local currency side by side with our FCI.
- ✓ Great advantage of our system is that each nation can apply for a license to use the FCI as their local currency with all rights to determine and manipulate fiscal controls as they wish. Agreed printing levels can be issued.
- ✓ There are no spillovers or domino effects. We are not a nation and every country can peg their currency against this FCI.
- ✓ Our system ensures global stability as we have a holistic approach working together to stabilize the world by banning wars, weapons etc. Tomorrow's World Order will act as a central body that is independent of all nations and is unlike the IMF we are against loans and structural adjustment programs or anything that sink people into debt and strips away their national sovereignty of which we think are the triggers of all the problems we have.
- ✓ Global debt stands above $244 trillion, and we think this system is obsolete. So, we propose a new system of dealing with old debt and banning national loans. Why get a loan

selling your soul to the devil if you are a sovereign nation with printing rights.

- ✓ We strongly believe that for seventy years the system has taken the wrong road of adjusting whatever money is there in the economy without thinking about creating new money. Growth as in a human body that needs constant food is achieved only through constant new printing of money. All other suggestions aren't true as seventy years have proved.
- ✓ I personally believe that Newton's Third Law apply in economic and financial sector as well; that every act be a force, a transaction or measure has an equal and opposite effect. This is true if you look at the Triffin Dilemma. Any actions by the country whose currency is used as the reserve currency will have an opposite effect to those using their currency as a reserve currency. So, there are spillovers to other areas and it's just adjusting the money that is already in the economy.
- ✓ Our thinking is that the country whose currency is being used by all as a reserve currency will gain what has been 'lost' by some countries who are using their currency as reserves or trading with them, etc. So, any gains of one country means losses of another. What has been happening with discouragements to printing new money and reliance on loans from the IMF was just a matter of shifting resources and wealth from one area to the other?
- ✓ Our plans are to increase global wealth to levels never seen before and this is only through printing of new money.
- ✓ Each 'sovereign' nation must as our law dictates print fresh money continuously for the next five years. The money they already have is not for servicing debt or for things that don't generate profits etc. but new money is to be used for servicing debt and consumables. We want to change developing nations into developed and developed into super developed.

- ✓ Our GRB will act as a control for excess money and not to flood the economy with new money but a careful planned system that creates savings for each and every nation as they print to deposit their local currencies with our GRB and in return get the equivalent in FCIs that is already global and used by every nation.
- ✓ We have a system to deal with debt. All current global debt to be treated as having a depreciation aspect rather than appreciating one. So, our system will treat current debt as depreciating over time with say a loss of 50% in value for the first year giving incentives for nations to payoff and start afresh. The second year a 40% depreciation rate, then 30%, then 20 and lastly 10% with the remainder written off. After six years no nation will be in debt all global debt will have been written off.
- ✓ But if it's debt that arose due to printing new money that is owed to local citizens of that nation then that is a different scenario. The system creates a situation through printing new money that will see the people need to be bailed-out. It is the government's responsibility to bail-out its citizens and not banks through new loans or mortgages or new capital. This new money will have lower interest rates and depreciating aspects that, over time the offset rule will be used to clear the debt owed by the government to its people when it printed new money with the new bail-outs of citizens.
- ✓ National debt through printing new money is part and parcel of the road to wealth and must not be feared but an effective way of dealing with it is needed.
- ✓ External debt owed to IMF and other nations must be feared and banned as it carries a sovereignty risk in that a nation can be forced to lose its powers of printing new money and controlling the fiscal and monetary aspects. It can be held to ransom as it might default and in most cases the lender has a huge arsenal of nukes which he uses to lend you in the

first place on the condition that if you fail to pay back, you will be sanctioned, etc.
- ✓ It's government's responsibility to be forever indebted to its citizens, and this is achieved through printing new money. Every time a government prints money it increases the value of its citizens and the wealth of its country considering that the money is not exported abroad, lost, misused, etc.
- ✓ A debt default reserve account must be created that will act the same way as a Provisional Depreciation account. This will be a Provisional loan default account with money stored in it to deal with debt defaults. A percentage of new printed money must be set aside into this account and when citizens can't pay, they must not be let to lose the wealth already accumulated but for the government to intervene fast and write off the debt after a certain period has lapsed.
- ✓ The idea is that of a government that is forever indebted to its people and this is achieved through printing money. And printing money must be a continuous process until certain levels have been reached. We have a system that works as it creates huge national wealth in terms of local currency deposits to our GRB and we will work hard to stimulate trade using the reserves to provide extra services the nation would otherwise not afford.
- ✓ We have a greater role to play as the global central focus of development and wealth. We are responsible for creating the extra 'supply' globally using the world's deposits to attract multinationals who can provide a supply of goods to meet the huge demand caused by new money.
- ✓ We arrange global skilled workforce using a percentage of the deposits as agreed to do whatever it takes to fight hyperinflation and stimulate global growth and wealth to a new never seen before level.
- ✓ Do you know that the most advanced nations are heavily in debt. These nations print money continuously and rely on

other nations to provide the extra supply needed to squash hyperinflation. So, to us these big few nations are like parasites to grow they depend on others for everything while discouraging growth elsewhere apart from their areas hence the developing nations has remained as developing for seventy years and only the developed nations are improving.

- ✓ Given that situation we think it is important that sovereignty be recognized as superior and critical to solving global problems and as the only hinge-pin to increased global wealth.
- ✓ Why we are saying that our FCI is to be used side by side with local currency is because this will help solve all of today's global problems. All countries will still have rights to use and influence their own currency, manipulating this for a competitive advantage e.g. devaluing local currencies to boost exports. Other countries buy in local cheaper currencies and then convert this to FCI, and a country will still use our FCI as well but not adjusting the price of these as prices are free-floating. The benefits will be achieved through currency manipulation.
- ✓ Using both currencies with ours which is independent of any nation will solve the problems of the Euro and reliance on another nation's currency as reserves while recognizing each nation's sovereignty and rights to control their destiny through fiscal measures.
- ✓ Tourists to any country might travel using the FCIs which is global so trade is still fast and even cheaper and all international transactions, investments etc. can be conducted in FCIs.
- ✓ Countries have rights to peg their currencies against the FCI to control their economy. So, this system ensures uniqueness and sovereignty while creating a fast way of transacting globally.

To reiterate here our system encourages generating new money and savings the only correct way through printing and depositing the new money in our GRB where we incentives nations to keep printing and depositing through paying out interest rates in FCIs.

- ✓ Our currency the FCI through the new printed money deposit scheme means it will exchange with all global currency this means a free-floating economy where there is no protectionism.
- ✓ Money manipulation techniques like devaluations are country specific and used to boost the economy and are not forced but optional the Beggar-thy-Neighbor devaluations don't apply here.
- ✓ No global adjustments only optional country specific, creating a free and fair environment.
- ✓ A sound political climate and huge confidence and a build-up of trust into the system but trust based on facts as our system is clear and transparent. They trust the system not just like now through faith but through a system that is robust and fit for the purpose.
- ✓ Countries can use the notion of the Hot Money Flows [HMF] where if they don't export much, they can attract investors by increasing interest rates of the local currency while cushioning the effects of HMF through our FCI. This can cushion against liquidity problems too.
- ✓ To encourage savings, we pay interest using the FCI on all savings.
- ✓ Overtime we will encourage nations to keep our FCI in their own national reserve-stockpiles in their own countries and use their local currency to boost trade and have a competitive edge over others while pushing the value of our money through upward pressure as local supplies of FCI available to trade are reduced.

- ✓ We as the central body TWO will only regulate rather than control so it's fair for everyone there is still competition and a nation's skills will determine success or stagnating.
- ✓ The greatest advantage of our system is that as we are not linked to any nation, our SRGC will be stable but valued as it will exchange with all global currencies something never seen before. A new era a new system that creates and keeps wealth.
- ✓ It will be illegal through our laws that a nation focuses on balancing books at the expense of its people. It's better to have an unbalanced balance sheet but increased value and wealth of your citizens.
- ✓ Our goal is to set new standards and new ways of doing things and take all mankind to levels never seen before. The idea being that if you are holding reserves in huge quantities of another's currency, they can easily print extra money reducing all your reserves to nothing. But our currency means you have the peace of mind that our money will remain the same ideally, we encourage printing new money in your own currency but exchange this for our FCIs.

THE CURRENT PROBLEMS AND OUR SOLUTIONS.

The current system has failed and is obsolete and only a new system can replace it hence our FCI. This is the only currency that is independent of any nation and is a solution to the Triffin Dilemma which I believe is the root of most of today's global problems.

Triffin Dilemma.

The Triffin dilemma or Triffin paradox is the conflict of economic interests that arises between short-term domestic and long-term international objectives for countries whose currencies serve as global reserve currencies. [Wikipedia.]

FutureGoldCoin

This is the only currency to solve reliance on another country's currency as the SRGC. Use of another country's currency as reserves has the domino effect or the spillover effect that can threaten global stability if the country concerned has say a huge balance of payments deficit problem. In most cases monetary and fiscal measures to correct domestic economy of the country whose currency is used as the reserve might have opposite and or equal effects that can trigger financial crises globally. Printing of new money will have an inflationary effect that spill to all those using that currency.

We as the new global leader TWO we believe the whole system established in the 1940s is now obsolete and our system is the perfect system for today's problems. For over seventy years now still the problems then are still the problems now.

Role of A Nation's Sovereignty as the Key to Success.

Our system believes and gives respect to national sovereignty as the only means to solving all current issues. Since with national sovereignty you have the only true way of creating wealth that will solve balance of payments, global deficit, global debt, unemployment, economic and financial issues among other things. Tomorrow's World Order strongly believe that the only solution is through a sovereignty guaranteed right: the right to print fresh new money without worrying about loan repayments and interest to pay. It's the only way to wealth. The current system is there to screw every country on earth but benefit a few. Only printing new money is the route to wealth and solving today's global issues but it's not just a case of printing money, that is where we come in because hyperinflation and general inflation are animals hard to tame but we have mastered the skills and I will tell you how. But first why FCI.

FutureGoldCoin is a digital currency together with our system and comprehensive approach will change the world as we know it today from global debt to huge national savings and global wealth. Our system and this FCI will provide;

- ✓ A fast and secure way to carry out global transactions.
- ✓ A way of reducing transactions costs greatly globally.
- ✓ Reduce major fluctuation risks.
- ✓ Help to boost trade globally.
- ✓ Help all nations generate huge savings and the needed new money to solve their problems.
- ✓ A huge helper in fighting hyperinflation and normal inflation.
- ✓ Will eliminate the Triffin Dilemma so that a country will stand by itself and its monetary skills will determine success rather than derailed by external forces.
- ✓ Will not take away the sovereignty of any country which is the only way to be self-sufficient and the road to wealth, with the current system whenever a country uses another's as a reserve currency it automatically loses this sovereignty and the ability to control its fiscal planning e.g. devaluing the currency to increase exports. It relies on adjustments by the country whose reserve currency is in use and therefore technically under it.

A Lack of Global Leadership.

Any system without a strong leadership is doomed. A system needs a global leader to lead it, to defend it and to protect it. This is the only way to safeguard and guarantee tomorrow hence the rise of Tomorrow's World Order.

There is a lack of a global leadership interested in a new system that solves all current global problems. We believe that as a people we are working below optimal levels. We can do much to improve living standards and the quality of life. There is no one else with a vision that will lead mankind out of poverty and all world problems. We believe there are solutions and we just need the right leadership to spearhead the journey toward a new chapter in mankind's history.

The Current System is Obsolete and Therefore Not Fit for Purpose.

We believe that all global and national problems arise due to the current system which was developed soon after the war and seventy years down the line we are still using the same system despite numerous crashes from financial crises to other economic problems and global debt that stands over $244 trillion triggering poverty, inequalities, economic problems, high unemployment levels globally and above all political instabilities in terms of wars. We believe that all the problems at hand from economic, social, political, financial and environmental are a result of a dysfunctional system that has crashed so many times. This we believe we're pointers for a need for change but mankind being mankind is unwilling to change and would rather just fix the current system when a new system can easily reverse all the problems. A system that can easily be implemented and improve the life as we know it today. We as a people are working below optimal levels. We can do better. If a system crashes, it means it need a total new system. In this case it's not a matter of just an upgrade. Why? This is because the system has crashed so many times that even fixing it is just delaying the inevitable. The main reason is not that the people don't know it, no. They do but they lack a Single Reserve Global Currency to solve all that. A currency strong enough to safeguard all nations' wealth. To fight all fiscal problems, like inflation, hyperinflation, deflation, etc.

The main issue is that humanity has been stuck in the defensive stages where they spend a huge proportion of the budget on defense; the military and weapons. We believe that mankind should be heading out of this stage or should have already done that. Therefore;

- this is wasting a lot of resources on weapons when global living standards are mediocre to poor. These resources can be used elsewhere to boost development and humanity's life.
- wars and weapons conflict with our laws. We have our laws that can never be breached or overridden without paying the consequences.
- we believe that everyone has a right to life. You might think this is the case right now, but the sad fact is that it is not. These laws can be overridden in favor of say national security, etc. A leader can kill thousands of women and children on national security grounds and get away with it. A leader or a nation or a gang or cult can murder thousands of innocent victims on humanitarian grounds and get away with it. Our laws are comprehensive closing all loopholes and making sure that no innocent people will die needlessly. We shall hold everyone to account and punish them harshly if they breach these laws.
- We believe that everyone has a right to self-defense. Currently these laws are overridden by other global laws coined to make it easy to stripe these rights away and punish those who have rights to defend themselves. A nation might try to match the threats at hand e.g. if being attacked

or threatened by a gang who belong to other cults and who use extreme force or weapons like Weapons of Mass Destruction as threats to steal or colonize sovereign nations. In these cases, it will be unreasonable for a nation under attack to try to match the level of threat. A nation in this case can successfully use the right to self-defense to justify say need to enrich uranium as the attackers have the Weapons of Mass Destruction (WMDs) themselves in form of nukes which they use to rob others instead of paying a fair price.

We believe all this is happening because there is a lack of a SRGC that will address all the problems at hand. We believe this is the major global problem. Our SRGC in FutureGoldCoin and Calycoin will make it easy to empower all sovereign nations to have enough money and national savings to be able to pay a fair market price. It is a fact nevertheless a sad one that the current thinking is that of making weapons cheaply and then use these weapons to get whatever they want.

I reiterate here as you will see why we are saying humanity has failed to think and rely on defense as a way of getting everything they want. The idea is to make weapons cheaply and then use the weapons to take resources at gunpoint. Mankind's thinking is still barbaric. I can't blame them as this is the only way mankind is accustomed to. A tried and tested method one that has worked over the past 2000 years. Since the beginning weapons and defense determined the survival of any nation. But hey that was 2000 years ago, and mankind was justified. The dinosaurs and other cannibal tribes of the medieval were a menace. Mankind had to be prepared to fight and self-defend. But open your eyes now it's the twenty-first century everyone wants to be a friend. Past wars' traumas have made all of us know pain and now everyone would rather Network and Cooperate the way it should be.

- As a people we can't afford to waste resources on things we don't need like weapons and the military. All these resources must be immediately diverted towards humanity's ever-growing huge population and better living standards.
- We must now change in line with changing needs. Our laws have banned wars and weapons manufacturing, dealings or trading of any kind all round the world. Disarmament will begin at a specified date. Above all current weapons have been replaced by digital and even with cyber weapons that are hidden, fast and cheaper and have mass murder properties.
- We have noted also that because of a lack of a SRGC mankind has relied on weapons and wars to fetch scare fossil fuel resources. We believe that all the last four to five wars or invasions were for resources or territorial growth mainly oil, simply because a nation has nationalized its oil reserves. We have seen it as a common practice that if nations run into debt and to minimize national bills, they tend to find cheaper things. Everyone knows oil depletes a nation's resources. If money is running out we need cheaper resources but for things like oil where there are no effective alternatives then it's reasonable to make cheaper weapons and use these cheaper weapons to extract or force down oil prices through wars and modern day colonization where a puppet government is put in place benefiting foreign investors as it is a condition for the puppet government to lax laws and provide favorable conditions for huge multinational companies and increase production to avoid the long petrol queues, etc.
- No matter how harsh and inhumane this sound this is a reasonable tactic that is if you are in debt or need to

save the little money the country has. It's a sound business model. Make cheaper things than use these to get expensive ones.

Our Plan.

- ✓ Our plan is to solve all these global problems and we strongly believe it is through provision of a strong SRGC in the FutureGoldCoin and Calycoin.
- ✓ A guaranteed way to make every sovereign nation on earth rich and have enough savings and monetary reserves enough to buy resources like oil at any market price. We strongly believe that a lack of a new system to global finances is the problem but we as Tomorrow's World Order have provided such a system and a Single Global Reserve Currency to eliminate all the problems without fears of hyperinflation and political instability.

Comprehensive Approach.

We have a comprehensive way to deal with all these issues;

Laws.

- ✓ First, we believe for all this to work the notion of sovereignty is to be given the greatest respect and status it deserves, and the rest will follow. It is this sheer recognition and acknowledgement that sovereignty of a nation plays an important role in eliminating all national problems hence global ones too. For as far as history can takes us back people and nations have gone to wars to either make or destroy this simple yet paramount idea of a nation's sovereignty. They know without sovereignty a nation is useless and can never solve its problems. The problems we have today are there because sovereignty has been

tampered with or not fully understood that nations are sinking in debt and manipulated when they can become very rich and self-reliant. Most have resorted to loans from the International Monetary Fund when they should not.
- ✓ Our laws place emphasis on this idea and protects individual nations and make them believe that it's being sovereign that makes them rich.

Ensuring the Right Leadership and Safeguarding the System from External Forces.

- ✓ Those in favor of the current system are the only ones benefiting from it killing innocent women and children to get whatever they want. We say no to inferior thinking and our laws are the only way to safeguard the future of every woman and child on earth. We need a just system that is appreciated and observed globally. A system that protects the weak and vulnerable yet the most valuable assets of any nation. Laws to deal with corruption and ensure that the system works. Laws to deal with dictatorship and evil gangs or cults who now use weapons, fear and intimidation tactics to abuse and rob people in the process kill women and children as a provocative stance to justify invasions and wars with hidden objective to take resources and at the same time carry out a Colony Collapse Strategy to eliminate 'threats to global peace and stability' but a genocide tendency to remove potential opposers and defenders of the defenseless; women and children who get killed through illegal wars needlessly.

The Financial System.

- ✓ We have a digital currency that has two main components. A macro-level currency that will be used as the Single Global

Reserve Currency called FutureGoldCoin. It is a digital currency and will act alongside a nation's own currency. This will be the global reserve currency. I know most use the US$ as the reserve and we are going to show you why this is the reason why global debt is above $244 trillion and why we have all the financial crises, we have through the domino effect. Using the US dollar as the reserve currency will link the whole globe to the US's skills or no skills of dealing with fiscal policies. I know the US Fed system has done a great job to carry everyone and build global wealthy but sometimes unforeseen circumstances like the 9/11 attacks can happen and trigger the global financial collapse. Our system will see to it that it's one nation for itself and Tomorrow's World Order for us all. We are sovereign in our own right and can print our own money. Set our laws and enforce these. We are not tied to any nation. Every nation that adopts our global digital currency will make it theirs in that we will provide the rights to printing, fiscal management and planning and monitoring something you can't get right now using the US$ as a global reserve currency. All nations will apply for a license to use our currency and might pay a small fee.

Global Reserve Bank. [GRB]

- ✓ Our plan goes beyond just providing a Single Reserve Global Currency but also a Global Reserve Bank that will help fight global and national debt and eliminate all the problems we have of poverty, unemployment, poor living standards, uneven wealth and a lack of a secure savings bank that can't be confiscated.
- ✓ The current system has used all laws at their disposal to steal and keep people in poverty through terrorist laws that confiscate assets just like robbing the savings of small nations. We have seen this with Sudan just after 9/11 with its

- savings in US banks frozen and taken and distributed to the victims.
- ✓ Our system will provide a global savings bank which I will explain later, each nation according to our laws and system must deposit regular and exponential savings that we as Tomorrow's World Order will keep making sure a nation will have wealth in perpetuity.
- ✓ Interest will be paid on savings but as our FutureGoldCoin and or Calycoin. We will hold the savings of every nation and we shall agree with nations concerned to use some towards development of that specific nation providing services they would not otherwise get. We can use the savings to link that nation globally. We shall use these savings to building border airports all over the globe that will speed globalization's Networking and Cooperation. We shall provide a global identity system that is fast and instant and ideally digital that can give results fast to speed up travel, etc.

Dealing with Current Debt.

- ✓ The current system was created by a few who must gain tremendously from it through global loans, etc. It is not a coincidence that global debt stands at $244 trillion. This is the way the current system is designed to hold everyone as ransom and crash a nation's sovereignty and sinking it in debt. It is a clever plan one that benefits a few nations mainly the former founders in that only these countries will grow at the expense of others. Only these nations will see improvement over decades while the others are sunk with debt ending up losing their sovereignty as they became puppets with a government appointed by the invaders or lenders of the loans. The current system stampedes on a nation's sovereignty by trading their freedom with loans.

Nukes in the Hands of a Few But Banning Everyone Else.

- ✓ The system has justified the making of things we are saying are Weapons of Mass Destruction and therefore banned. What justifies these nations making and keeping nukes and use these to force others to abandon any uranium enrichment or possession of nukes? A few nations have seen it fit to make and hold WMDs we are all saying are against modern international laws and using these to make money and loan it out using these nukes as an enforcement method encase the nation fails to pay.

Sovereignty Risk and Conflicts with Our Laws.

- ✓ Borrowing from external sources puts any nation under the risk of being attacked in case it defaults putting all its residence at risk. This conflict with our laws the rights to be sovereign, the right to life, the right to self-defend and right to a good quality of life. Global loans of the IMF etc. means a heightened sovereign risk as whatever happens is dictated. You must meet certain conditions and implement certain structural adjustments that all impact on our laws and a nation's ability to develop and solve its economic woes. The structural adjustments will only make a country be able to solve the problem the loans were taken to solve but opening reverse yet similar problems. In other words, this only shift problems and focus from one area to another or in the worst cases cause worse problems.

Real Idea Behind the IMF and Global Laws.

- ✓ The idea from the past 2000 years is to build a big empire through fighting wars to be able to print money and create a supply to provide goods and services to match the increase supply of money hence demand of goods in order to fight hyperinflation. I explained that the only way a nation can grow naturally without accumulating debt or increasing sovereign risk or breaking our laws is through printing fresh new money. No matter how good or best the economist or treasuring or the Federal system is without new money growth is just a dream. It's like a human body without extra food you can never grow. You might reshuffle all you like but growth is only through new food intake. We believe this is the only true way. All this idea about austerity, best economics or better policies is just child play, misconceptions and trickery or manipulation so that a few bigger four or more nations have markets and sources of goods and demand as well to avoid hyperinflation.

Empowering Every Nation by Providing the Best Framework to Reduce and Eliminate Side Effects of Our Growth Method.

- ✓ Our vital critical notion from the beginning is that without national sovereignty no nation can ever increase national wealth to levels never seen before. For the past seventy years a lot of factors have played to undermine a nation's sovereignty and ability to solve their problems. Only through sovereignty can a nation take control of its destined and increase wealth. Printing of money, the only source of economic growth and wealth is linked to sovereignty. All sovereign nations can print their own money. Use of another nation's reserve currency limits your own sovereignty hence the inability to influence your own destiny.
- ✓ Our aim is to empower everyone to shift them from developing to developed and from developed to most advanced and in the end all to superior nations with wealth never experienced anywhere.

- ✓ Our currency will play a critical role and whether nations succeed or fail will depend on their use of our currency and system. Our currency will solve all problems that affect growth when a country prints money: it fights hyperinflation as a country must use two currencies ours and theirs.
- ✓ Prices during hyperinflation can be determined by our currency as theirs might lose value as prices change many times per day.
- ✓ Offers a currency used by hundreds of other nations and still maintains the nation's value. Printing own currency means the currency having no value to other countries who would be using a different currency. But having and using our currencies will mean the value of the new money will be increased, and the wealth increased too.
- ✓ In worst-case scenarios they can stop their currency for ours until they have eliminated hyperinflation and resume when things get better.

Creating Global Savings.

- ✓ Our plan is to ask all nations to print new money continuously but all the new money to be deposited in our bank as it will be in their own currency making this their savings and we in turn will convert that currency to ours and give them our currency and advised how best to inject the new money into the economy without flooding the economy.
- ✓ We then use their savings to generate interest for them over time. Every nation will have savings that they just keep say for five years without taking yet still printing and depositing. This will be reviewed say every five years to see if the nation can benefit from withdrawing the savings to boost the economy and wealth.
- ✓ Our plan is to shift nations from the current level to never seen before heights of wealthy and living standards. We

believe the current system crashed many years ago and only a new system and way of thinking is needed.
- ✓ Our system relies on the natural way things should be. The current system is to increase inequality and keep the rich richer at the expense of everyone else. Empowering all these nations to enrich themselves and improve the living standards of its inhabitants should be their sole existence.
- ✓ No sovereign nation can ever be in debt again. Fight all this talk about austerity and excellent balance sheets. We have laws that make it illegal to focus at balancing the budget and books at the expense of your people.

Sole Reason for Government's Existence.

- ✓ We believe all governments are elected by the people and governments exist to serve the people. Therefore, governments should be indebted to its people forever and in perpetuity. This is very important as this will be the justification for printing new money.

The Value of Printing Money.

- ✓ Every time a nation prints money it creates extra value at no cost at all. The new money is not to be repaid back as loans neither does a government pay interest on printed money. When it prints money, the government owes its people and not externals and every time this happens the wealth and value of its people increases. So, the government by printing money it owes its people this new money. The time it injects money into the economy wealth is created and everything boosted. New money means new capital, new loans, new mortgages, jobs, developments etc. and a sense of economic stability and political stability too all which will enhance a country's wealth and value and attract even more foreign investment.

Government Mandate to Bail-out Its People.

- ✓ Printing money makes governments owe their people. So, as we know new money can create all issues with inflation and hyperinflation, most of which will be dealt with our new digital currency but for some time this can't be avoided as it is part and parcel of growth. There shall come a time when the people will face difficulties. Banks will tighten lending etc. and the economy might start contracting and people might have difficulties repaying the loans, mortgages, etc. In this case the people start defaulting owing money. It must be the government's responsibility to create more new money through printing and bail-out the people and not wait to bail-out the banks only as the current thinking.
- ✓ Our laws and thinking will make governments realize that there are there simply to be indebted to its people. Initially the government through printing new money must owe its people. When people take loans, mortgages and other investments a time will come when they are in debt and start owing money. It is and must be the government's duty to intervene and bail-out the people by printing new fresh money and deposit this with us and we give them our global currency and we can still provide loans, mortgages using this money free of interest to people of the nation who deposited money and or the government then provide loans to its people interest free to avoid them losing their wealth and getting possessions repossessed.
- ✓ The government of any nation must see bailing-out its people as its duty. No wealth must be lost due to non-repayments and defaulting, etc. Just as the government can easily print new money it should also easily write off the debt

owed by its people where it can be proved that unless doing so can result in accumulated wealth being lost. New loans, re-mortgages etc. must be easily made accessible, and the debt owed, or loans still owed depreciated over time instead of being appreciated.

Perpetual Indebtedness.

- ✓ But again, it is not yet over. I explained that every time the government prints money it prints the money from nowhere without bonds all it must acknowledge is the fact that it owes the people every time it prints new money. Ideally to provide new loans the government must use its own money or savings we hold in our reserves which they have deposited. This is the only way they will stop or eliminate the I owe you a debt. But they printed new money, so the vicious cycle starts again. So forever if the source of money is through printing new money the government will forever be indebted to its people and this also means continuous perpetual wealth and growth of its people. We will discourage using their money reserves and savings they already must service debt etc. but to print new money and keep owing its people to never seen before wealth.

Forever Growth and Building of Wealth.

- ✓ Our plan from the word go is to make it easy for any nation and the globe to be able to grow its wealth exponentially to levels never seen before. The current system has made it a vicious cycle where wealth is gathered and lost and gathered again with the same process being repeated. In the end when they die, their wealth is destroyed, and a few transferred to the living relatives. Our aim is to maintain the wealth or level of growth from generation to generation.

Dealing with Debt. The First Rule is to Offset it.

- ✓ I explained earlier on that it is the government's duty as a sovereign nation to print money. Secondly this duty enables it to owe its people this new printed money. It is also part of the system that at one point or another the people will sink into debt and owe banks, the government, etc. To offset the initial 'government I owe you' to its people created by printing money the government must pay the 'debt' it owes these people by bailing-out all of them. So, it will mean the government has to print new money to pay or bail-out the people through provision of loans that will be written off in the end. So, when people are in debt and the government lend them money that will offset each other so that if debt owed by both: the government to the people and the people to the government through accepting loans will cancel each other so that no one owes anyone.
- ✓ Wealth is not destroyed as the government stepped in before repossession and provided loans to be written off to cancel the government's 'I owe you'. In the end the "I owe you debt on both sides is zero."
- ✓ Every nation, especially the big four the most advanced ones rely on debt and have the biggest percentage of debt by far. To grow you must be in debt of some kind otherwise where would you get the new money to see growth. It's all through printing and for the rest of the world it's debt they owe these through different institutions like the IMF and other direct loans in cash or kind.

Two Kinds of Debt.

- ✓ Global and National debt is in two forms.

Government's 'I owe You' Through Printing New Money.

- ✓ The biggest debt of the most developed nations is debt through printing more money and or owing other nations as they exchange and trade. This is what is called external debt.
- ✓ External debt shift wealth from locals to externals and must be discouraged at all cost as it conflicts with our laws. Owing another nation is like selling your soul to the devil it's irrecoverable or at a cost. You can be sanctioned and attacked, and your sovereignty limited. This is the debt that is hard to eliminate as the lender might not what to write off that debt and can keep it for years while still growing instead of depreciating.
- ✓ Debt owed to locals by governments through printing is easily written off or offset.

Dealing with External Debt.

- ✓ We have laws that will treat global debt as depreciating in that we shall assume all national or debt to externals etc. as having a depreciation attribute in that it reduces in value over time. The current system is like that of loan sharks with debt ever-growing to enormous levels and laws that see to it that that is the case. Our laws are designed to eliminate debt and enhance savings through encouraging nations to print new money gradually without taking the savings. So, we shall decide with everyone who is owed to consider writing off that debt or reduce the debt over say five years with huge depreciation rates at the beginning to give people chances of paying off before eventually writing it off.

The Debt Plan.

- ✓ First year current debt to lose say 30 to 50%, followed by 20%, then 15%, then 10% and finally by 5%. After say six years if the nation hasn't paid then write it off.
- ✓ There shall never be a new debt again if a nation is sovereign.

Use of Printed Money.

- ✓ Money already in the system is not for servicing debt or other things not central to the development of the economy. The idea is to bring in fresh money to solve current problems. For things that have zero profits or no income generating capabilities to be serviced through new printed money only. Projects that generate money can be funded through both existing and new money. The idea is not to crash the system or cause bottlenecks.

Print Extra Cash to Act as A Buffer to Loan Defaulting.

- ✓ The idea is to regard a certain percentage as irrecoverable bad debt and use the new money to offset such debt. A certain percentage is set aside in a buffer account and taken out whenever bad irrecoverable debt is written off.

Five-Year Plan Gradually Printing of Money.

- ✓ Our plan is to increase savings and tackle current problems and this is only through printing of fresh new money. For the coming five years all nations must print money gradually increasing and depositing this money in our bank and exchanging the value with our money the FCI and Calycoin (CLC). Our FCI and CLC will be injected into the economy to boost growth and development without causing other problems associated with hyperinflation. No nation at that time will take external loans. It shall be a law to print as advised by us on quantities so as not to flood your own economy.

Supporting Packages.

- ✓ Tomorrow's World Order shall use the deposited loans and a percentage to help every nation create the extra supply that might be needed due to an increase in demand spearheaded by new money. We shall use a percentage of the deposited savings or interests to develop modern and good quality infrastructure like airports at every border in addition to current airports. Increase connectivity by linking the whole globe through fast internet and transport systems.
- ✓ Use our laws to build and maintain political stability globally to fight hyperinflation. Train and make excellent talent that can be hired globally available at short notice.
- ✓ Use the savings to establish global companies that will provide and improve infrastructure etc. to link the whole globe together to help all nations develop and advance.
- ✓ Create even more jobs as we change and force institutions our ways of thinking. The idea is to ban institutions that are creating or worsening the current situation like the IMF etc. unless if they can change and take new roles. Loans for nations will be banned, etc. We will have banned wars too and weapons manufacturing and trading. The only way to get resources at market prices would be to print new money and use our system to avoid hyperinflation and steer growth.
- ✓ I have pointed out that oil is the main reason for wars. It's just a fossil fuel and to help stop wars forever and make inferior thinking a thing of the past we will ban use of fossil fuels for vehicles like cars, busses, trains, planes, etc. Every nation will have new money which they can easily print to

- ✓ fund research and development and come up with their own renewable, cheaper and clean fuels like electricity.
- ✓ Everyone will have access to new money, and we will keep their savings too. Wars over fuels are banned and stopped for good. In turn this will help tackle climate change. All fumes etc. and pollution eliminated as current vehicle e.g. cars phased out globally by a certain date. New clean environment and breathing air that is in line with our laws the right to a good quality of life shall be the norm. All noisy vehicles will be replaced by new silent and fuel-efficient ones.
- ✓ We shall use the savings and new money to develop new materials that are strong as steel but lightweight and easily available. All modern metal vehicles etc. to be banned and phased out by a certain date.
- ✓ All buildings never to use fossil fuels but only renewable clean and cheap alternatives. Some building materials to be banned as well, etc.
- ✓ Our laws to tackle human rights abuses and dictatorship issues. Make everyone accountable and answerable to us.
- ✓ The military will be challenged to do the opposite of everything they do now. If they kill, we shall challenge them to create life. If they destroy, we shall challenge them to build, etc. The current thinking must change, and the current system must be considered as crashed and when a system has crashed only a new system must replace it. Our system is the only true answer.

Ban Sanctions.

- Another issue that can derail our plans is sanctions. We stand against sanctions of all forms and ban these and enforce our ban through very harsh laws. First this is because sanctions conflicts with the rights to life, right to self-defense and right to a good quality of life. Secondly sanctions are there just to weaken the target nation or leader so that it, he or she can bargain in the end in favor of the sanction-imposer. I think they are barbaric and cruel and as they target the innocent and powerless the act of imposing sanctions on another sovereign nation is an act of provocation enticing others to revenge and therefore justify the sanction-imposer's stance that of justifying wars. An act of sanctions is an act against all mankind as it invokes our Article 1 that state that an attack on the weak, the defensiveness and voiceless, yet very valuable members of the society is an attack on all of us. The idea and reason behind sanctions is to kill innocent women and children to anger the targeted government or to damage its credibility. If someone can kill their women and children in broad daylight and they can't do anything about that what kind of government is that? That will start internal turmoil and uprising that will be used as the reason to invade on humanitarian grounds. The reason being that a few of the opposition will instead attack the 'useless government' as they let women and children get killed on their watch and do nothing. It's like ball-rolling. The sanction-imposer kills the innocent with the aim that someone in that country will understand the motive and fight the government. In turn this government will already be angry and humiliated that they have been proved to be weak this in turn will make them pass the anger to these rebels and end up using the harshest punishment e.g. chemical weapons to get some sympathy over the death of innocent women and children on their watch or simply use extreme force to show power and be feared. When that happens the sanctions-imposer 'has humanitarian

grounds' as with this current situation to invade and attack that government.
- We are against such manipulation and evil trickery methods of using the innocent yet valuable members of the society as bargaining tools and bait. We strongly condemn such practices because the terrorists use the exact same method by killing the innocent women, children and men to push their agendas.
- So, we don't see any differences between a terrorist and a sanction-imposer. They are the same thing and we shall treat them the same way.
- Fourthly sanctions can destroy a nation's wealth and economy. Printing money when sanctions are imposed has only one outcome total failure of that economy. We view this as a cheap way of robbing others and killing innocent people something we stand strong against.

✓ Improve global wealth and spearhead development while increasing living standards to never seen before new heights.

✓ Our plan is to shift humanity from defensive economies to the next stage of development of Networking and Cooperation. We believe mankind has been wasteful spending huge sums global on military around $1,9 trillion global in 2019. This money can be used elsewhere where it really matters.

Problem at Hand.

- All global problems are due to a lack of a Single Global Reserve Currency called FutureGoldCoin [FCI] and the Calycoin [CLC]. A currency that will be used globally by all nations and one that will provide a platform to solve all current problems. A Single Global Reserve Currency will solve all problems of huge global debt, loans, global poverty, global unemployment, global economic hardships, lack of globalization, inequality between developed and developing nations, lack of capital to spearhead development, all financial crisis, repossessions, even political instability and global wars and reliance on weapons to solve everything. There is a predicament hard to solve without this Single Currency Global Reserves in that for every sovereign nation the only way to solve all the mentioned problems and more is through a constant supply of new money. This is the only natural and cheaper way through printing; and ensuring a healthy cash supply enough to solve all global problems, yet no one knows how best to tame and eliminate that thing called hyperinflation. We Tomorrow's World Order has the answer, and it's through our idea and plan of the Single Global Reserve Currency in the FCI AND CLC.

- ✓ There is no other plan that will guarantee global wealth.
- ✓ First a plan that provides leadership to protect the system. A new system needs a global leader to defend it and stand for it. A great leadership can guarantee the future of that system. You can have a perfect system but with no one to fight for it it's useless as it can be banned, frozen, or outlawed without any one standing for it. Tomorrow's World Order is a global political party that is sovereign with rights to print our own currency and laws and to make sure that our laws are followed globally. We have powers to enforce these as our laws are already international laws or regulations of which no one is to breach. All digital money without a great leader to defend it is at risk but with Tomorrow's World Order you have a genuine leader who is determined and eager to solve global problems if that means doing away with the current system so be it. We have seen the current system crash and become obsolete with age. Mind you the system has been there since the mid-1940s and worse we still have the issues they had then, wars, weapons, poverty, inequality,

unemployment, global debt, a dysfunctional system, political issues and breaking of all laws known to humans. We still have prevalent cases of torture, modern day slavery, human rights abuses, piracy, hacking, invasion of privacy etc. and to make things worse it's the government apparatus who are responsible and worst culprits of all rights abuses. The system has grown to huge levels with the major players exerting enormous power through membership to cults that they don't even listen to their own laws and courts etc. It's like in a gangland where weapons are used to rule and get people what they want with innocent women and children tricked to think that current institutions can really stop the war. Tricked into being given a false sense of security with institutions like the United Nations Security Council claiming to stop global wars yet be given the rights to enter countries like Iraq to inspect claims of WMDs and actually declare that there were no WMDs but yet fail to stop or even delay a war. Our stance is that two wrongs will never make a right. We must be proactive and safeguard the lives of innocent women and children people who are given a false sense of security until the day they die from bombs and bullets. This is a thing of the past. We shall drag to court all these institutions who gave these victims a false sense of security but watch them die. Our laws have introduced new concepts that will close loopholes being used to evade justice.

Empathy Clause.

- We shall assess empathy to see if say the sanctions-imposer or warmonger ever considered the notion of empathy or rather acted with undue regard to human life putting the lives of these people in danger recklessly and something, he would never do to people not remote to him. A classic example is the world standing still if one kid dies in the West through violence i.e. guns etc. and when 500 000 die abroad through their bombs and missiles no one gives a damn.

Humanitarian Grounds.

- It shall never suffice as a justification for invading or attacking a sovereign nation. Our aim is to uphold through laws every nation's sovereign rights. A sovereign nation shall never be attacked, and no grounds shall suffice. Humanitarian grounds shall never be enough; especially if the country concerned has imposed sanctions in the past against the target nation. Sanctions that killed or caused unnecessary hardship to women and children. These shall be the benchmarks of any humanitarian claim. Women and children shall be the litmus test. What you do to these shall reflect your true motives. No way you can succeed on humanitarian grounds or 'Responsibility to Act' when you have brought unnecessary hardship to these people before and even killed some directly or indirectly. There is no collateral damage when it comes to women and children. You must and will be held accountable.

Widen Scope of Punishment.

- Under these empathy and humanitarian grounds, we shall add another criterion. Showing no empathy with women and children of others will cause the law to add yours as well to the punishment. We shall assume that your actions can and will reflect how you feel about your own women and children. If you don't love yours or feel nothing towards them, then you can go on killing others. The idea here is that if you love yours it also means loving others because what you do to others will be done to yours too. It goes beyond the current thinking in that your acts can bring risk to your own as well. If you love them, then act morally and value others as well.

- All this is possible with a new and true global leader with everyone at heart in there to solve issues and not to make money or tackle hyperinflation at the expense of the whole world. Trickery and devious practices will be punished harshly as well. All governments to act responsibly and honest and improving the lives of its people.

Lack of Understanding of What is Really Needed in Life.

- Our laws punish and drags to court 'some smarty governments' who focuses on balancing balance sheets on paper when their people are in dire poor living conditions. I emphasized above that we will impose minimum global standards after everyone has printed enough money to boost wealth. Governments that lack focus and engage in austerity measures at the expense of its law-abiding citizens are breaking our laws. Rather be in debt and having a wealth country with happy people than have a perfect balance sheet. Again, I reiterate that governments are in power to be indebted forever to their people to boost wealth.

✓ A plan that will guarantee elimination and reduction of global debt.
✓ A plan that will guarantee a perpetual exponential growth of global and national savings reserves.
✓ A plan that will eliminate all financial crisis forever.
✓ A plan that will guarantee the ever-growing wealth of a nation and the globe.
✓ A plan to eliminate unemployment globally.
✓ A plan to eliminate stagnating economies and boost all economies globally.
✓ A plan that improves living standards exponentially globally.
✓ A plan to eliminate reliance on fossil fuels through new alternate sources.

- ✓ A plan that will provide peace globally as our laws will ban wars globally for real and not like the current system.
- ✓ A plan that will ban weapons manufacturing globally, arms dealing and trading, etc. A plan to create a weapon-free world.
- ✓ A plan to reduce the defense budgets and phase this out progressively.
- ✓ A plan banning all sanctions globally.
- ✓ A plan to deal with global debt treating this as depreciation or giving it a depreciation attribute instead of treating it as wealth that increase in value.
- ✓ Banning of global loans for nations. All sovereign nations to utilize our system and laws and print as the only easy free and cheap way to new fresh money.
- ✓ A plan that will help all global leaders on critical paths to decision making and evolve most institutions and practices as these have been there since the 1940s and honestly have achieved little to nothing and now, we think the current system is obsolete and not fit for the purpose. A new system is the answer.
- ✓ A plan to provide a stable political, social, financial and economic and environment where trust in governments is at the highest with the government acknowledging that they are there to be indebted to the people and to serve them.
- ✓ A plan that let everyone involved know that it's a mutual arrangement to benefit all with the government with a responsibility to bail-out its people rather than banks.
- ✓ A plan to encourage better fiscal practices and laws than are there to see growth and development never witnessed before.
- ✓ A plan that involves the government and the people to be accountable and transparent with our laws on the side fighting corruption, etc.

- ✓ A plan that will ban making and use of bio-engineered, digital and cyber weapons etc. as watermarks to protect their people or currency, etc. Lacing of valuables like a nation's money is against our laws. All these can only be achieved through chipping people; implanting chips into the body without consent usually at birth and this violates all laws known to mankind and conflicts with the right to life. The right to self-defense how can you if you are tracked getting ambushed etc. and conflicts with the right to a good quality of life. These things use radiation etc. and electromagnetic nerve stimulation is as good as hacking stripping away all rights. All these abuses in most cases are by the government apparatus disguised as national security, immigration control and a way of commanding the nation.
- ✓ All issues are so cumbersome that only a new system will rewrite history and put an end to all this. Only our system will guarantee a safe future with:
  - no wars.
  - no weapons.
  - equal rights for all.
  - no torture.
  - no hacking even by governments.
  - no slavery or re-colonization of any kind.
  - upholding of the rule of law.
  - effective laws than bans a lot of harmful things like fossil fuels that have led to   wars on top of that polluting the environment.
  - better future fiscal and monetary planning
  - better political, financial, social and economic stability.
  - a New World Order a new beginning. The main idea is that the current system is very old if it were a person, he or she would be a pensioner [no disrespect] but the challenges we are facing today requires new thinking and ways of doing things. After all the same problems exist even after seventy plus years.

- ☐ Third Type Error.
  - The current system is designed for other reasons other than solving global issues. This is true in that the big four or so nations behind all this system knew they had to print money to grow. But printing is a trick job as it in most cases trigger hyperinflation. So how to tackle this hyperinflation? Create institutions just pretend they are there to solve current problems to trick and deceive people but just as holding reserves for the big nations to take off surplus new money by keeping these to fight hyperinflation. That can explain the presence of the same issues as seventy years ago and why most of these institutions like the IMF cannot help the nations in need but hold $billion in reserves.
  - We have institutions or cults like NATO acting as the last form of defense for the two leading attackers who wage war on anyone who criticize them stirring others to make or think about getting nuclear weapons to match the threat at hand as these nations group and grow using military force as a way to get what they want and command obedience. At the same time using things like Article 5 to give a member immunity and grant backing without merit that that nation has done nothing wrong to provoke criticism. This is in line with issues where governments might outsource terrorism to justify other critical war-contingency objectives with the aim to go to war to eliminate future risks and threats to ' peace and security' but whose peace as they kill innocent women and children?

The Causal-Effect Relationship.

- We believe that all the problems we have today are a result of a lack of SRGC that will solve all these problems. There is a direct relationship of all current issues with the lack of such a currency. The current system that relies on another nation's currency as the single reserve for the whole globe is flawed in that the domino effect will drag everyone down. Unforeseen circumstances might cause financial collapse unlike if the SRGC is owned by us an independent unbiased sovereign entity not linked to any government so not politically influenced by any governments. The current system relies on reserves of another country that belongs to a regional cult that has articles prohibiting losing sight of the ball of enhancing that cult alone and not everyone. This is a regional cult with limited global focus. It is reasonable to argue that their goals and objectives are for the betterment of them alone at the expense of everyone. Who don't believe that a regional cult that has a requirement like in Article 8 demanding that all members favor the cult and must not do things contrary to the goals of the cult and above all should not do things that will jeopardize its existence? In such circumstances trying to play a global leader can only anger some with serious consequences. We are the only hope of an unbiased global power with true goals for global peace, empowerment and making every nation and its citizens very rich. So the problems are directly related to the lack of this single reserve global currency that will act as the currency of all nations to use as a backup to be used together with their local currency to fight hyperinflation as printing new money is the only certified option one we recommend.

Recap: The Solution in Brief.

- ✓ A global digital currency with two aspects one for macro-level bulky or government functions for all everyday transactions payments and deposits etc. called FutureGoldCoin. [FCI] Secondly a micro-level peer-to-peer currency that will be in circulation aiding the macro-level FCI that is called the Calycoin [CLC] a digital currency. The FCI will act and shall be the SRGC. Our main idea is to use this FCI mainly but supported by the CLC together with a nation's currency as the fiscal currencies in use.

Printing Rights and Licensing for Fiscal Monetary Measures.

- ✓ Tomorrow's World order as a sovereign global power have printing rights and shall allocate through license these rights to all nations to be able to print their money and be in control of fiscal and monetary aspects as well so they are in a better position to control their wealth and development.

The Currency as A Hyperinflation Fighter.

- ✓ Printing new money means hyperinflation if nothing is in place. Our currency will fight hyperinflation. We shall encourage the printing of own currency then deposit this money into our reserve bank. In turn we will give them the equivalent in FCI and CLC which they will inject into the economy to cushion against hyperinflation. The currency is a global currency that will easily be accepted globally making sure that the value of printed money is not lost and making sure that the new money will add value and not lower the currency's value.
- ✓ FCI and CLC prices can be used to determine say the value of products as the local currencies can lose value quickly due to increased demand so prices can change every day. Nations will be able to tackle

- hyperinflation by using a combination of their own currency and our FCI.
- ✓ The system will for the first time enable all governments to have huge perpetual savings held in our reserve bank which can generate more interest which they have access to after certain periods. Increased wealth than debt now. Increased wealth and living standards. We can use the savings to further global growth and development by choosing and or forming huge global investment companies that can increase the supply of products in relation to increase new money. That will attract more investment etc. with our laws, framework and platform we provide stability to all nations and globally creating a conducive environment necessary for growth and development. We shall use the reserves and develop better alternatives to everything we do with aims to cleaner renewable cheaper sources of everything to increase wealth and quality of life and prolong life to levels never achieved before.

Levels Never Achieved Before.

- ✓ This is the key element of everything we are going to do. We have seen what the current system can do, and we are saying that it's not enough. For seventy years we have experienced small changes unless if the effect was adverse. We need a system that guarantees huge changes in beneficial attributes. We need growth to levels never thought of. Our plans are ambitious and only us can do that and our system is the only system that can help mankind achieve that. We have bold and broad plans for all mankind. We are arguing that the current system favors a few when we can all achieve great. So, first things first we need this currency and we have tokens as explained in the Methodology part below.

- ✓ We are not going to be anonymous like the Satoshis who have private ambitions etc. and for fear of repressions would rather hide their identities, etc. We are transparent as we represent the whole world and argue that there is a way a new way of solving all these issues without anyone suffering loses. Our plan is for all mankind as we are going to solve all the problems and take the world to new levels never seen before. We have a strong leadership in Tomorrow's World Order and believe we have the right system to see our plans through. Initially we shall use tokens to generate cash to build our system which will have its own digital currency and blockchain that will be augmented with a strong and secure reserve bank both for the digital money and the new printed currencies from all over the world as we shall act as the only global reserve where all deposit will be made to empower and boost every nation making them richer as these savings will be held without being taken out as there is no need to as printing will continue in perpetuity. So, money is needed hence we shall officially launch a coin or token offering to raise capital to implement and start solving global debt.

Your Part.

- ✓ I am excited that if you are still reading that means I have convinced you already that this is the only way to solve global issues and the prospects and returns of our plans are never seen before or experienced before. Imagine all nations without debt and encouraged through our laws to generate and accumulate wealth to tackle every kind of problem we have today. Imagine a world where no matter what price of a commodity we will be able to pay for it. Unlike the current situation that makes your leaders make cheaper weapons with the aim to use the cheaper weapons to gather expensive resources like oil through wars and invasions. Imagine no queues for commodities like petrol. Imagine every nation with its way of making and doing things cheaper and cleaner with renewable energies, materials, etc. If there is money everything is easy. No wars or fighting but stiff competition or other beneficial fighting etc. in the name of being the best at something and not killing innocent women and children to lower world oil prices. Imagine a world without current polluting vehicles with heavy metals and all the noise but with clean fiber-glass-like materials which are light and clean to the environment. Where quality of life is better, and governments live to make their people very rich and not cheat or trick them into debt. A world free from debt but with huge savings in our reserve bank. All these are just the global and national benefits what about your benefits as an investor?

Benefits to You the Investor or Supporter.

- ✓ First, we have minted already the tokens as a digital cryptocurrency to raise the funds to help us see our plans through.

- ✓ The project is real, and we see real potential and a need to act fast and be sure that we provide a better tomorrow for us and for our kids. We have seen what the current system can do and to be honest after seventy years we are sure that we have seen the best it can offer and honestly the system crashed years ago, and we ignored calls and warnings for change.

We view the current system as a broken fuse amp. Now after too many crashes the fuse amp is irreparable and irreplaceable and what the current governments have done is replaced the fuse put in place for our safety to protect the whole system from burning in case of a fire with a solid wire that will keep the fires burning forever once the trigger has been activated and we don't want that situation and what this can mean as it can mean the end of humanity as we know it today. Imagine still making weapons etc. while the world is becoming friendly; with North Korea and the US now on talking terms yet the budget for the military keeps growing. $1,7 trillion is a huge sum and this money can be used to deal with population and global growth.

Reliance on Wars as A Solution to All Problem.

- ✓ Main reason we are stuck in defensive economies is that this is the only tried and trusted method to solve global problems. For the past 2000 years wars have rebalanced the ecosystem by eliminating over surplus and created the perfect ideal environment the system can accommodate. Your leaders have used wars to reduce the government's debt and the expenditure bill in terms of the soldier's salaries to balance things. Most military interventions are triggered by missing funds and unbalanced budgets etc. Wars have solved this issue easily. All you must do is just start a war. By the time the war has ended millions of people including soldiers will have died. Then you have fewer soldiers and other people on the payroll. Fewer population pressures, new contracts of weapons deal to boost the economy, etc.

- ✓ Wars gives everyone every reason and justification. Huge military budget and health budgets all are justified easily when there is a war simply because all these services and institutions like the health care are a result of past wars, so they must benefit if same situations are created. New military weapons contracts, etc. are drafted after a war. Need for new weapons manufacturing and budgets are increased accordingly. A boom to the economy.
- ✓ New printed money is sent abroad to fight hyperinflation, etc. The current economy is related to wars to some extended and depends on wars or their planning in terms of war-contingency plans to mitigate future threats and therefore justifies investing in military related economic activities driving economies, etc. This has caused many nations relying on a global super power like the US for loans handouts etc. and reliance on its currency as a reserve something we are sure now is the root of global issues with the 2007 financial problems having a source in the US. The situation can easily be manipulated by those behind this in their favor that everyone else's sovereignty is stripped away and all rights to print money that impacts on abilities to be self-sufficient. In exchange they become puppets that have no power to influence their destiny therefore be sunk down with loans with high interest rates and conditions that make one put the lives of all its people at risk. Something we are strongly saying is against what we stand for as this conflict with our laws. The current system lacks a single reserve and digital global currency that is not dependent on wars to spearhead development.

PRODUCT/SERVICE/METHODOLOGY.

- ✓ I have highlighted the methodology already above how we are going to solve all these problems and here I will go into the specifics of the methodology.

Raising Initial Capital to Kick Start the Project.

- ✓ We have already minted our digital tokens that we will use to raise initial funds to see our plans through. All the people interested can buy our tokens or exchange cash that is fiat or in digital currency like Bitcoin or Ethereum etc. for these tokens. The tokens have been made already and are ready with all security features in place giving everyone a peace of mind. We are serious about global peace and justice and we are tired of complaining about the current leaders and governments and campaigning when we can establish our own system as we like it and convince everyone even the politicians that this is the only way forward. We have done the hard work now we know what we want and how we can get there.

Your Role. Support Our Initial Token Offering.

- ✓ Only you can see our dreams come true and this is through getting involved in every sense of the word. Spread the news and chat with friends and challenge the current norm and make suggestions we are open to your views and would want you to be involved and take part as well. The future belongs to you as well and wouldn't you want to be part of this new movement of change where we make the changes rather than complaining about the leadership that is there.

How Many Tokens for the Initial Offering?

- ✓ Our plans are cumbersome and just saying a figure might not be enough, but we believe we must start somewhere and go on from there. We are also confident because we are looking at the whole world and it will be easy to involve the world and let those who believe in us contribute by buying our tokens now so that we create a true SRGC and establish physical reserve buildings everywhere for holding the new printed money. I think the best way is to establish a tier with targets rises as soon as we achieve them.

Initial Offerings

- ✓ Huge gains initially as the token price verses say Bitcoin or Ether will be very low offering our team a real investment and reasons to work hard for you. So initially there are new bargains to be made with price-cuts of around 60% of the value at launch.
- ✓ Tier I.
  Token 100 000 000.
  Aiming to raise between $10 million and above to start working on our project and hiring staff to see the dream a reality.
- ✓ Tier II.
  Token 500 000 000.
  Aiming to raise anything above $ 50 million.
- ✓ The Tier III.
  Another 250 000 000 to 500 000 000 tokens put for sale.
  Aiming to raise $75 to $ 250 million.

With own network taking effect globally introducing players to be partners etc. to oversee the project in individual nations.
- ✓ Tier IV.
  As we expand globally, we expect to raise even more money to start creating reserves to be exchanged with printed new money and we can offer.
  Tokens 1 000 000 000.
  Aiming to raise $250 to $700 million plus.

Recall we have adopted a holistic approach that means laws, a system that works and connections globally to create reserves and, in the end, physical reserves for holding new printed individual nation's money. All these will present their problems at every stage of development that we might need more resources than we are suggesting here so our plans will be revisited as we go too.

Pre-Sale Offerings.

- ✓ Token value going to 40% of true value to still attract more people to support us and buy huge quantities.

  We shall offer more tokens in billions.

  Tokens 10 000 000 000 offered in pre-sale for all aspects of the project that is seen as part of the initial; critical path phase.

  Aim is to start creating reserves to be exchanged with printed new currencies and to circulate globally. A certain percentage for security and further development of the system to make sure as a global leader we can provide global standards everywhere.

Initial Coin Offerings Kick Off.

Token value will be 30% off the final price of the tokens to still attract investors and maintain the interest as well. Launching of this will be global and to speed up the process we will offer even more tokens.

- ✓ Tier I.

    Token 100 000 000 000.

Aiming to raise $1 billion in reserve funds and a certain percentage being used for further security, unforeseen circumstances, development, improvement and securing the system against all external forces. Advertising and publications can and might cost us more as we will need heavily advertising globally to attract more people. Some funds for recruitment of people on a temporary basis globally to create the biggest buzz ever.

- ✓ Tier II.

    Token 500 000 000 000

    Aiming to raise $2 billion plus mainly for reserves.

- ✓ Tier III.

    Token 1000 000 000 000.

    As we can get will be very welcome.

What Are the Benefits to You?

- ✓ The best news is that we are a global force with global ideas and targets which means our plans are universal and includes everyone. Imagine a global currency with the need to increase everyone's wealth the only natural way to do so is through printing money. People and nations will be able to pay a small fee and get rid of debt for good. All surely considering the benefits mentioned above will without doubt make everyone to anticipate the increase in value of such a currency and they will buy our tokens. Imagine if Bitcoin is just for an anonymous underground or hiding group or person what more if this is linked to a great leadership that will guarantee tomorrow.

Guaranteed Tomorrow.

- ✓ Bitcoin owners are anonymous, and this could be a reason why it hasn't taken off as most people anticipated. There were huge talks of a $100 000 Bitcoin between now and next year December and Bitcoin only started rising to above $10 000 two or three years ago since 2017 before that it was below $6 000 for most of the years. The unpredictability and a lack of transparencies in the leadership can cast doubt in the future value of the currency. We as a global movement offer a form of security that somehow your investment is guaranteed, and we are behind this and that our aims are universal that will attract more supporters. We aim to tackle things current governments are having headaches with like inflation, hyperinflation, national debt, unemployment, lack of supply to match demand triggered by surplus new money. Lack of savings for most of global nations so we can act as advisers that in turn can make our system and plans be appealing to many even to current governments who might become part of our system without too much convincing. We all share a common ground of finding ways to make the world a better place. No one can be expected to be against us unless it's the same people causing all these problems for selfish personal gains. Our laws will break them down.
- ✓ I reiterate that we are sovereign in our right and no leader is above our laws. We have relied on international law under

the Jus Cogens that are laws that are universal like our first laws; rights to life and a good quality of life. Everyone is familiar with these laws. What we have done is to prioritize these laws and make sure that no one will have justifications for breaking them without getting sunk by our laws. No one can argue otherwise. No wars, weapons, immigration or national security can override these laws. These laws will make humans be the priority and everything else to follow suit.

- ✓ No one has immunity we have stripped these off. We must use our Article 1 to lobby and use global collective justice to punish our law breakers and drag Presidents and Prime Ministers to court while still in office. We shall evolve the justice system by making the whole system be a twenty-four hour service with the digital part operating all the time especially at night where cases can be logged into the digital system at any time but processed automatically at night and forwarded to judges etc. during the day who will then look at the cases etc. that is if human judgment is required. For most we shall use digital judgment in that we shall provide the laws as digital and let everyone on earth read and confirm that the laws have been read and a time lag or time stamp is created showing date and time even place when someone did confirm reading these laws and this to be used as a reference point and where violations are observed the system can automatically offer ways for the person to address that breach. Ignorance of not knowing the laws will not suffice as everyone will have had access to the laws to read, understand and confirm these. Complicated cases to be dealt with by human judges.
- ✓ Above all this we are removing all time limits to laws which states when all laws can expire, and cases be brought to court. Currently some have time limits of 3 to 6 months and most government apparatus take advantage and chip people at birth so that they are under the 'death row' from the day

they were born with watermarks loaded into them as a population control method or immigration one as they have huge aging population that does harm to the nations finances, etc. Some governments hack their people and wait for the time period to launch a successful case to expire before they start torturing them.

- ✓ Our research has shown that this is a common practice by some nations that abuse as the abuse is by the state which is institutionalized and systematic perpetuate by governments agents and when the victims complain they are further abused and tortured into taking drugs like heroin or cocaine as a way to cover up for what these governments did to them. Therefore, we banned and removed time limits. Any case can be brought to court if the accused person is still alive. This guarantees a fair and just system with immunity removed and everyone facing justice. A new start and a new beginning as reconciliation and a better world can start if there is a form of balance. Wars, sectoral violations, torture, genocide, violations of human rights all can easily be solved by our approach. Most people will be able to complain about abuse and stop things like secret government torture where they think they can easily blame the victims as drug addicts and cover the real issue.
- ✓ All this will restore trust in governments and in the system that everyone will see the benefits and subscribe by becoming part and parcel as they all will benefit. Imagine where government have to Bail-out people including you and not banks. Imagine a situation where your savings are protected forever and only you can reduce its value. A system geared to benefit everyone is rare, yet we have ours as I have elaborated above to solve all global problems.
- ✓ Our laws will fight corruption too which is a real problem and the major trigger of hyperinflation. If we mint or print new money that ends up abroad or in a few people's huge

pockets, then the whole system is rendered useless. So, we have laws to fight this corruption. People must trust the government and expect it to be transparent and fair. Our laws will close all loopholes and make the government accountable and increase the people's wealth and improve political stability too.
- ✓ Our holistic or comprehensive approach is the best prerequisite for a successful plan and hence future wealth. The value of our tokens will increase exponentially and by the time we have gone global they could be worth more even better than Bitcoin.
- ✓ So, investment in our Tokens the; FCI and CLC is the best move and makes it easy to never work again but to sit, relax and trust in our system for a comprehensive solution to all your needs.
- ✓ The trust and political, financial, social and economic environment created will surely enhance the value of our digital currency.
- ✓ So, invest! Buy our Tokens and be part of this great new movement. You can always be involved in several ways.

   ➢ Spread message on Facebook, Twitter, Reddit, Telegraph, Instagram, LinkedIn, Tumbler, etc.

NEW SINGLE RESERVE GLOBAL CURRENCY

FutureGoldCoin [FCI].

- ✓ Predictability a Sure Way to Success.

Predictability and Stability are very paramount to the success of any campaign. People would invest even if the idea is not that great simply because they have nothing to lose, they will get their investment capital back. Stability gives people peace of mind to quench all fears of instability and corruption etc. and losing their money and having hopes of gaining something in return. If chances are that they will get something back, they are willing to invest, etc.

Calycoin [CLC].

- ✓ Get in Get Involved with Something Special.

People are willing to get involved and be part of something special and this is that one special thing. Ending all future wars, giving everyone back that sense of security and a framework that work to fight wars, unnecessary deaths of women and children, elimination of poverty, empowerment of every nation and individuals with global advice and guidance is something unique and truly special. It's unreasonable for any men and women not to appreciate our system.

Tomorrow's World Order [TWO]

- ✓ Universal Appeal.

It is a fact that issues with universal appeal are easily adopted and appreciated worldwide. There has been growing concerns with global issues like wars, needlessly killings of women and children, the rise of human rights activists and NGOs, etc. People related to all issues central to this and to find a way of solving such a problem and provide a financial aspect to that has a global appeal and the impact is great and obviously make the project worthwhile. I bet there are billions of people fighting for what we have highlighted but without a perfect plan like ours of addressing the issues by solving the real problems. Top find a perfect way to solve all global problems that guarantees future wealth of everyone has global appeal and makes the project as a real investment and as such we will always have people to subscribe to our ideas and plans.

The only question is; when should you be part of this?

DETAILED DIGITAL CURRENCY INFORMATION.

✓ Our goal is to have our own blockchain with two digital currencies the FCI and the CLC. We aim to write perfect smart contracts; which are agreements between us Tomorrow's World Order and you our potential investors coming to some form of agreement that in the future you will have financial gains as our digital currency increases in value. Our digital currency has huge potential as it will act as a single reserve global currency. This means transacting with everyone in the world. Why?

✓ Simply because all nations must use our currency for holding their value and assets. We are not linked to any nation.

✓ We shall aim to perfect the smart contracts.

✓ Increase high levels of freedom.

✓ Increase transparency.

✓ We have challenges in that we will be dealing with all global currencies so scale if part and parcel of the system. This will be at macro-levels as capacity is enormous with huge volumes that will make the need to bundle transactions into bundles.

✓ Potential issues will arise due to the sheer size of the task at hand, but we shall be very proactive and try to anticipate issues beforehand.

Your Contributions to the Startups.

✓ Initial selling Pre-sale price to ETH shall be around 0.00004 to 0.0007 which is a cheaper way to raise the needed capital for the initial launching and promotion and for recruiting our team. It's a huge task so we shall require a lot of expertise to see us through and initial Pre-Sale is vital to us.
✓ The more you contribute the more tokens you shall get.
✓ There is no doubt the value of our token will increase as all nations in order to be competitive and boost exports to generate more of our SRGC they will have to stockpile our digital currency and this will put upward pressure on the currency making it scarce as compared to their currencies pushing the value even high.
✓ The fact that each country will be using our digital currency the FCI will only mean increased value. This is how our digital currency will even topple Bitcoin. Our Single Reserve Digital Global Currency as the name implies will act as the base reserve currency replacing the US$. The fact that it will be used

side by side with local currency simply means having the best of both worlds as with the Euro and the current system.
- ✓ Once nations are familiar with how our new system will work surely, they will subscribe to our ideas as this is the only way to solve all global problems. We have the answers but without your contributions it might be difficult. Once again this is bigger than Bitcoin or the US$. The moment you will understand how this will revolutionize the world we know today, the more you will see the impact as well this will have. Imagine a reserve currency pegged against all global currencies, the possibilities are endless.

Why you Must Invest Now and Buy Our Tokens the FCI.
- ✓ Benefits provided through smart contracts are out of this world. Our currency will be more popular than any currency now because this currency will solve all of today's problems with;
- ✓ Inflation which means every time the US print extra money anyone with US$ in reserves will find that their value will lose. But with ours no value is lost, and countries everywhere would love it as it stores and maintains the value. Another great advantage that will see the value of our token rise is the fact that every nation on earth will have to deposit their local currency in our Global Reserve Bank. Imagine us keeping everyone's savings? They print new money

and the money in local currencies is deposited with us. We then give them our digital currency the FCIs to use to fight inflation and hyperinflation but while still stimulating growth. Our currency's value as the reserve ideally will never be below and country all the time. To boost trade and exports etc. these countries have at one point must remove our FCIs and stockpile these to make them scarce and therefore increase their value so that their local currency becomes cheaper. This is what Bitcoins tries to achieve by burning some money with time to create that scarcity but Bitcoin is not a reserve currency and some rarely use this but for growth and prosperity all these nations if they don't use our digital currency hyperinflation will collapse their system. To prosper and even survive, they must enroll into our system.

✓ Stability and predictability will play a critical part to increase the value of our FCI digital currency as we are part of a phenomenon global movement to ban wars, weapons, needlessly killings of women and children etc. Everything we stand for has a global appeal, so our currency and model of thinking has already had billions of people behind our project. We mean business that in the end even the toughest tyrants will succumb as justice will prevail.

A Clear Roadmap.

Even Bitcoin has no clearer roadmap than ours. You must as well read my book: *Tomorrow's World Order.*

Pre-Sale.

- ✓ We have a holistic approach to current problems and in order to do all the laying of foundation we need to raise funds through Pre-Sale. So, get in get involved and contributed towards our project we accept all digital currencies that trade with Bitcoin and ETH. We take fiat as well simply find the links below and visit our websites and buy our tokens today.
- ✓ So far since we are dealing at a global level we have generated;
- ✓ 1 000 000 000 000 000 000 1 quadrillion tokens.
- ✓ With currently 2 000 000 in circulation.
- ✓ The Pre-Sale price to ETH could be between 0.0000004 to 0.00003.
- ✓ We need many people to be in our team almost in every country to establish our platform and deal with security and other issues.
- ✓ Our plan will ensure a constant supply of fresh new money through printing this in local currencies and changing this with our FCI that means there is always a demand for our money, and this will see our FCI increase in value in perpetuity. Above all, all nations must

hold our currency in their own reserves as this is the only reserve currency so there is a constant demand. The fact that they must stockpile this digital currency means upward pressures of our currency no matter what. Value to you will be exponential.
- ✓ Trust me it works I have been thinking about this for some time now. Everything Bitcoin is trying to do will come to our digital currency naturally.

Let's Compare the Growth-and-Value Increasing Tactics Between Bitcoin Strategies and Our FutureGoldCoin Currency.

- ✓ Bitcoin's maximum supply is just 21 million coins. This is understandable as a currency that is globally but not for everyone too much money will reduce its value in the long run.
- ✓ FutureGoldCoin has so far, a total supply of one quadrillion with the world reserve currency estimated to be $11,4 trillion in 2019 in foreign currency that can tell the issue at hand. Mind you our digital currency is not just for global reserves but also for global trade and transactions which means the current supply is in line with projected demand. Currently most countries shun the current single reserve currency for fear of losing out due to inflation. We have seen China introducing its own reserve currency the Renminbi but still that has issues just like the current reserve currency.

Our SRGC will solve all the problems and Tomorrow's World Order will put down the framework and foundation needed to see real growth and value over time.

- ✓ Bitcoin will burn some coins to create scarcity as a direct intervention tactic to increase its value.
- ✓ FutureGoldCoin will become scarce naturally as for nations to boost exports they will have to stockpile it as digital in their reserves and use the local currency only. This is for exports to become cheaper and make our currency the FCI dearer. The fact that it will fight hyperinflation will mean everyone needing it over their local currency and so supply is ever-growing.
- ✓ Above all printing money will be continuous for five years before we review the plan that means ever increasing demand triggered by new money. The system is naturally ever hungry there is no need to burn or create value by cutting numbers. A huge supply of new money will keep forcing demand upward hence the value too. So, our stimulation tactics are by-products of policies to boost growth and development. A clever way of going about things; a win-win situation.

So, Are with Us? Join and Contribute Today!

- ✓ Since our Five-Year-Money-Printing plan will be a law with everyone expected to print, inflation and hyperinflation will force all to use our FCI that will increase its value and status. In the end it will be trusted as it will have proved to be trustworthy.
- ✓ That also shows you the task at hand.
- ✓ We will need powerful systems that will require enormous power and computer systems.
- ✓ Heavy security and monitoring too.
- ✓ Huge launching cost as the message to be sent globally.
- ✓ There shall be the establishing of support bases in every country.
- ✓ In the long run we shall need a secure physical Reserve Bank to hold all printed new money. That will mean security and logistic challenges, but the benefits are out of this world. Imagine earning loads of money as returns at the same time solving global problems through;
- ✓ Banning wars, [mind you, current wars can happen even though the UNSEC claims to stop wars, but we are going to put down laws to stop war globally once and for all]
- ✓ Banning weapons manufacturing, etc.
- ✓ Saving future lives of women and children
- ✓ Banning sanctions globally.
- ✓ Introducing new laws to make the world a better place at the same increasing global

peace and stability with action on the ground not just talk as the past 70 years.
- ✓ Wouldn't you be proud of such a movement?
- ✓ Above all we are GLOBAL!!!

Distribution Scheme Percentage of Total Supply

Pre-Sale	20%
Founding team	20%
Early Investors	5%
Global	33%
National or Institutional Investors	17%
Reserves	2%
Incentives for Users	3%

CONCLUSIONS

- ✓ It all starts with us. We can't expect others to solve our issues. Here is a chance for every mankind to change things for the better. There is no doubt that the current system has crashed many years ago and that only a new system is the only answer. For seventy years they have devised and planned yet the system and situation hasn't changed. We are arguing that we can do better as a people. It is up to us to act and act we must act now. We can't leave things to chance. Institutions like the United Nations Security Council gives all women and kids false hopes of security by preaching of ending wars yet they have no powers themselves and are part and parcel of the corrupt system trading women and children's souls for lower priced resources globally like oil to avoid long queues at the fuel pumps, etc. We stand firm against such thinking and declare that humanity must change its thinking. We can change the world for the better and we can't do this alone. That is when you come in. Be part of this special movement and make the world a better place for everyone. It is easy and can be achieved but requires your commitment as well. What is the main problem is a lack of a Single Reserve Global Currency

[SRGC] to take humanity to the next level of development?

FACT: A lack of money makes today's leaders make cheaper weapons and then use these cheaper weapons to get them expensive things they can't afford like oil to affordable prices.

FACT: Our system creates enough money and savings that will make making cheaper weapons to get expensive resources look stupid as everyone will afford buying at any market price. We have put in place a system and framework to create enough money for everyone and fight hyperinflation at the same solving global problems. What is not to like there? What are you waiting for?

JOIN US TODAY!!

So, our currency the FCI is one that will make global transactions easy. A currency with a leader and a framework behind it to support and defend it and secure it to give everyone a sense of trust and predictability. Most digital currency lack that stability and or predictability that usually triggers growth and value in a digital currency. We declare that our already made tokens which we will exchange for other new ones once we have raised funds will have its own blockchain to make sure that everyone is a player and willing to contribute. Our SRGC and framework will;

- ✓ eliminate current global and national debt through methods suggested above like treating global debt as having a depreciating value instead of appreciating value. After certain years if not paid then the debt can be written off against a global debt fund reserve.
- ✓ Provide a Global Reserve Bank [GRB] where they can deposit new printed money and get our FCI in exchange instead. This stimulates savings and as an incentive to keep printing there is interest on savings. Our reserve bank will be the biggest with currencies of all nations to boost the wealth of these nations.
  This GRB will act as a money supply control mechanism removing extra money from the system while it earns interest as well at the same time fighting hyperinflation etc. and keeping everything stable. We will use the savings say a certain percentage to provide specialist functions e.g. multinationals that increase supply of goods in relation to greater demand due to new money.
- ✓ An independent reserve global currency will solve the Triffin Dilemma.
- ✓ A single global reserve currency will solve the Beggar-thy-Neighbor issue
- ✓ Our FCI will make payments faster and transaction cost very cheaper
- ✓ Will enable countries to manipulate many fiscal and monetary factors to spearhead development through devaluation, pegging and

HMF manipulations to attract more investors, etc.
- ✓ Our FCI must be used side by side with local currencies and nations be encouraged to stockpile our FCI to improve trade that will keep the supply of our FCI locally in short supply increasing the value of our FCI.
- ✓ No protectionist a free-floating system with our FCI exchanging with all global currencies through the savings deposit scheme.
- ✓ No adjustments associated with the IMF that only create a negative effect on the other side of the globe and other economic issues to the country concerned. We stand against adjustments but rely on dealing with debt and writing off this as the only way to guarantee exponential wealth and growth. We have laws to protect citizens' wealth and not let them lose this.
- ✓ Our system recognizes that it's a vicious cycle of generating cash, injecting this, boosting the economy and the extra surplus then creates more negative issues before the market starts contracting again wanting more cash injections. What has been happening is that the system was being let to crash and the process be start all over again. Our system recognizes that it's a mistake not to intervene to prevent crashing. Waiting for the system to crash first and solve it is the biggest mistake for the past seventy

years. All governments and our TWO must and will intervene to maintain wealth levels and keep injecting new money until desired growth and wealth is achieved. The government to intervene and Bail-out citizens and not banks since printing new money triggers an 'I owe you' situation with governments owing its citizens and not corporations like banks. To repay this 'I owe you debt' the government must bail-out the citizens and write off their debt over time and create at the beginning Provisional accounts for bad debt etc.

✓ Greater stability as we tackle most issues that can trigger hyperinflation and economic problems like sanctions imposed on a country fighting inflation. So, we banned all sanctions. Every nation is sovereign, and sanctions treats sovereign nations like kids who need to be grounded etc. Above all sanctions and other methods of adjustments are cruel and barbaric and used to kill women and children as a weakening took for a better bargain. We stand against such practices.

✓ Honestly in conclusion, the current system encourages one or two big nations to do what everyone else must be doing to grow and forbids everyone else to do just that but uses them to increase their new markets to supply extra goods to quench demand increased by printing new money. The system removes other's sovereignty and leaves them as dependents nations hence the lack of growth elsewhere, but hope is with us; A perfect solution to global problems, Tomorrow's World Order and our Single Reserve Global Digital Currency.

- ✓ It's up to you now.

Join Us!

Let's change the world for the better. It can be done. Never leave things to chance. Our system will work as we are doing this for all mankind and it's a global movement surely, we are destined to win. Get in on the winning side and be part of this great revolution a new chapter is imminent and inevitable.

Tomorrow's World Order.

BUY OUR TOKENS TODAY!

Visit https://www.futuregoldcoin.com

https://www.calycoin.com

I PROMISE YOU VALUE FOR YOUR INVESTMENT!

Thank You.

Mr. David Gomadza

Signed

07/08/2019

President

Tomorrow's World Order.

https://www.tomorrowsworldorder.com

info@tomorrowsworldorder.com

futuregoldcoin@inbox.lv

calycoin@inbox.lv

davidgomadza@hotmail.com

00447745900178

Telegraph https://t.me/davidg2077

Key Takeaways

- ✓ It is possible and can be done you just need the right framework and mind to appreciate our plans and methodology.
- ✓ It's only through us who can change things for the better.
- ✓ Above all what not to like making money while building a better tomorrow today.
- ✓ If not for yourself do it for your kids and all future generations.

JOIN, DONATE AND GET OUR DIGITAL CURRENCY.

Thank You in Advance.

Table of Abbreviations

GRB	Global Reserve Bank
HMF	Hot Money Flows
SRGC	Single Reserve Global Currency
TWO	Tomorrow's World Order
CLC	Calycoin
FCI	FutureGoldCoin
IMF	International Monetary Fund
NGO	Non-Governmental Organization
US	United States
WMD	Weapons of Mass Destruction

Tomorrow's World Order
by David Gomadza.

A Must Buy If You Are Serious About Solving Today's Global Problems.

A New Chapter. Change Is Imminent and Inevitable!

Are You Ready?

THE END

www.ingramcontent.com/pod-product-compliance
Lightning Source LLC
Chambersburg PA
CBHW022128170526
45157CB00004B/1790